T0080956

Spirituals

A Collection

Eleven arrangements for mixed voice choirs by **Richard Allain**

Novello

NOV955405
ISBN 1-84609-725-8

Music setting by Barnes Music Engraving.
Cover design by Michael Bell Design.
Back cover photograph of Richard Allain by Wojtek Wojnar.

Published in Great Britain by
NOVELLO PUBLISHING LIMITED
part of The Music Sales Group
Head office:
14-15, Berners Street, London W1T 3LJ, England.
Telephone: +44 (0)20 7612 7400
Fax: +44 (0)20 7612 7549
Sales & hire:
Music Sales Distribution Centre
Newmarket Road, Bury St Edmunds, Suffolk IP33 3YB, England.
Telephone: +44 (0)1284 702600
Fax: +44 (0)1284 768301

www.chesternovello.com

The Spirituals represent an extraordinary religious, social and musical legacy. They are among the most enduring examples of all vernacular art, and their appeal remains undiminished. These poignant expressions of joy and sorrow were crafted with the utmost simplicity and a noticeable absence of sentimentality.

As a musician and teacher I have always found inspiration in these melodies. The arrangements in this volume reflect my relationship with several choirs over the last decade. Some, including *Didn't My Lord Deliver Daniel*, were written for my own students for a newly formed school choir. Others, such as *Don't You Weep When I Am Gone*, were written for Mike Brewer and the extraordinary National Youth Choir of Great Britain, with whom I have enjoyed a close relationship for many years. Mindful of the variety of styles, musical forces and levels of difficulty, I hope that choirs large and small, amateur and professional will all find something suitable in this collection.

Richard Allain

for the *Mill Hill School Chamber Choir*

Didn't my Lord deliver Daniel?

Spiritual
arr. Richard Allain

* Parts shown as cue notes optional.

3

4

Dan - iel, why not e-ve-ry man?___ De-li-ver,

Dan - iel, why not e-ve-ry man?___ De-li-ver,

Dan - iel, why not e-ve-ry man?___

He-brew chil-dren from the fie-ry fur - nace, then why not e-ve-ry man?___

did-n't my Lord de - li-ver, did-n't my Lord de - li-ver, did-n't my Lord de - li-ver,

did-n't my Lord de - li-ver, did-n't my Lord de - li-ver, did-n't my Lord de - li-ver,

Did-n't my Lord de - li-ver, did-n't my Lord de - li-ver, did-n't my Lord de - li-ver,

De - li - ver, de - li - ver, de - li - ver,

Go down in de lonesome valley

Spiritual
arr. Richard Allain

* or semi-chorus

14

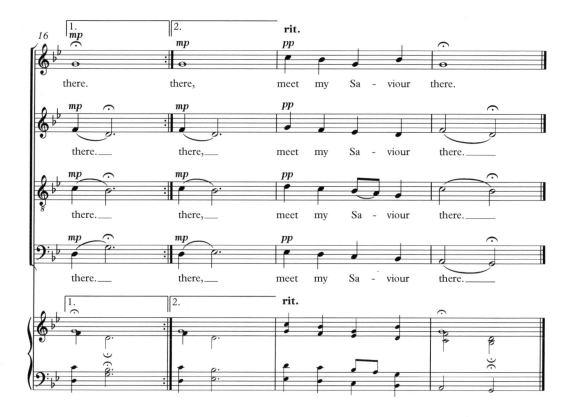

Walk together, children

Spiritual
arr. Richard Allain

This piece can be performed up a semitone.

walk to-ge-ther, chil-dren, don't__ you get wea-ry, walk to-ge-ther, chil-dren, don't

to-ge-ther, to-ge-ther, to-ge-ther, to-ge-ther, to-ge-ther, to-ge-ther,

to-ge-ther, to-ge-ther, to-ge-ther, to-ge-ther, to-ge-ther, to-ge-ther,

walk_____ to-ge-ther, walk_____ to-ge-ther, walk_____ to-ge-ther,

__ you get wea-ry there's a great day co-min' in the pro-mised land.

to-ge-ther, to-ge-ther, great day co-min', pro-mised land.

to-ge-ther, to-ge-ther, great day co-min', pro-mised land.

walk_____ to-ge-ther, great day co-min', pro-mised land.

26

walk to-ge-ther, chil-dren, don't__ you get wea-ry there's a great day co-min' in the

cresc.

to-ge-ther, to-ge-ther, to-ge-ther, to-ge-ther, great day co-min',

cresc.

to-ge-ther, to-ge-ther, to-ge-ther, to-ge-ther, great day co-min',

cresc.

walk_____ to-ge-ther, walk_____ to-ge-ther, great day co-min',

29

SOLO SOPRANO *mf*

When I was just a lit-tle child my Ma-ma said to me:

pro-mised land. I'll walk, ne-ver tire,_ I'll walk_

pro-mised land. I'll walk, ne-ver tire,_ I'll walk_

pro-mised land. I'll walk, ne-ver tire,_ I'll walk_

pro-mised land. *Thm bmm thm bmm thmm bmm thm bmm thm bmm thm bmm*

20

Go down, Moses

Spiritual
arr. Richard Allain

† May be performed down a tone.
* Solo optional

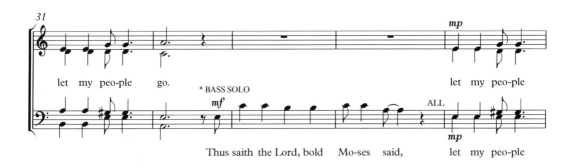

* Solo optional

Go down, Mo - ses, 'way down in E - gypt's lan', ____ tell_ ole ____

Pha - raoh, to let my peo - ple go. Go down, Mo-ses, 'way down in

E-gypt's lan', ____ tell ole ____ Pha - raoh, let my peo-ple, ____

to let my peo-ple, ____

Let my peo-ple, ____

let my peo-ple, ____

let my peo - ple go!

* If only SATB are available, this section to the end may be sung by 1st soprano, 1st alto, 1st tenor and 2nd bass.

for David Drummond and the London Oriana Choir

Were you there?

Spiritual
arr. Richard Allain

for NYTC

Gonna set down an' rest awhile

Spiritual
arr. and additional words by Richard Allain

38

For Mike Brewer & NYC

Don't you weep when I am gone

Spiritual
arr. Richard Allain

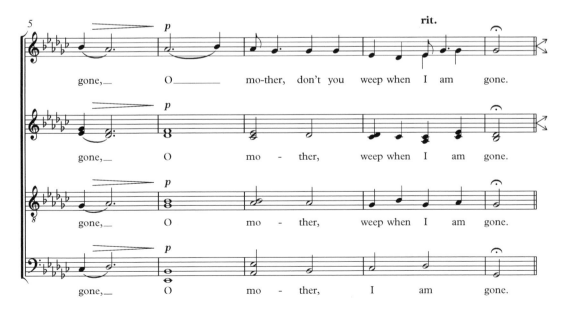

42

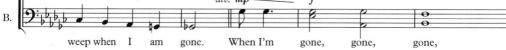

*originally commissioned by Susan Digby for Sir Willard White,
Laudibus and the Voices Foundation Children's Choir*

Scandalize' my name

Spiritual
arr. Richard Allain

54

for David Drummond and the London Oriana Choir

Steal Away

Spiritual
arr. Richard Allain

58

Commisioned by Susan Digby
for the Voices Foundation

'Tis me, O Lord

Spiritual
arr. Richard Allain

for 2 SATB choirs and semi-chorus or children's choir

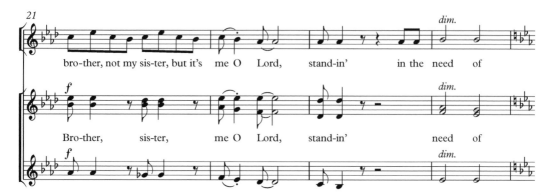

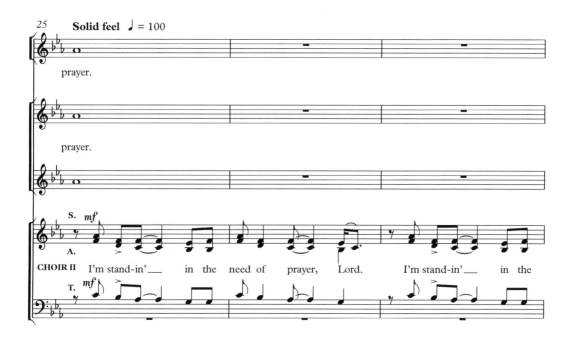

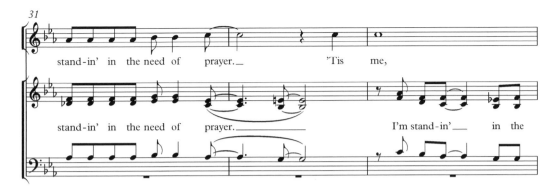

stand-in' in the need of prayer.___ 'Tis me, me,

stand-in' in the need of prayer._____ I'm stand-in'___ in the

I'm stand-in'___ in the

me O Lord, stand-in' in the need of prayer.___ Not my

need of prayer, Lord, stand-in' in the need of prayer.___

B. mf I'm

cresc.

dea-con, not my eld-er, but it's me O Lord, stand-in' in the need of prayer.

cresc.

I'm stand-in'___ in the need of prayer, Lord, stand-in' in the need of prayer.

cresc.

stand-in',_____ I'm stand-in',_____ I'm stand-in' in the need of prayer.

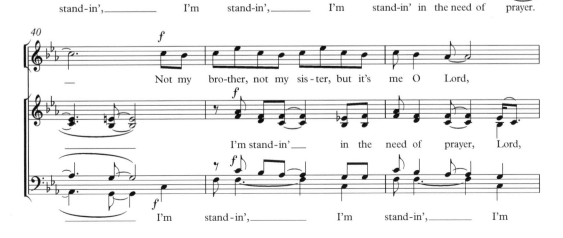

f

___ Not my bro-ther, not my sis-ter, but it's me O Lord,

f

I'm stand-in'___ in the need of prayer, Lord,

f

I'm stand-in',_____ I'm stand-in',_____ I'm

for Mike Brewer & the NYC Choirs

Give me Jesus

Spiritual
arr. Richard Allain

* Solos optional

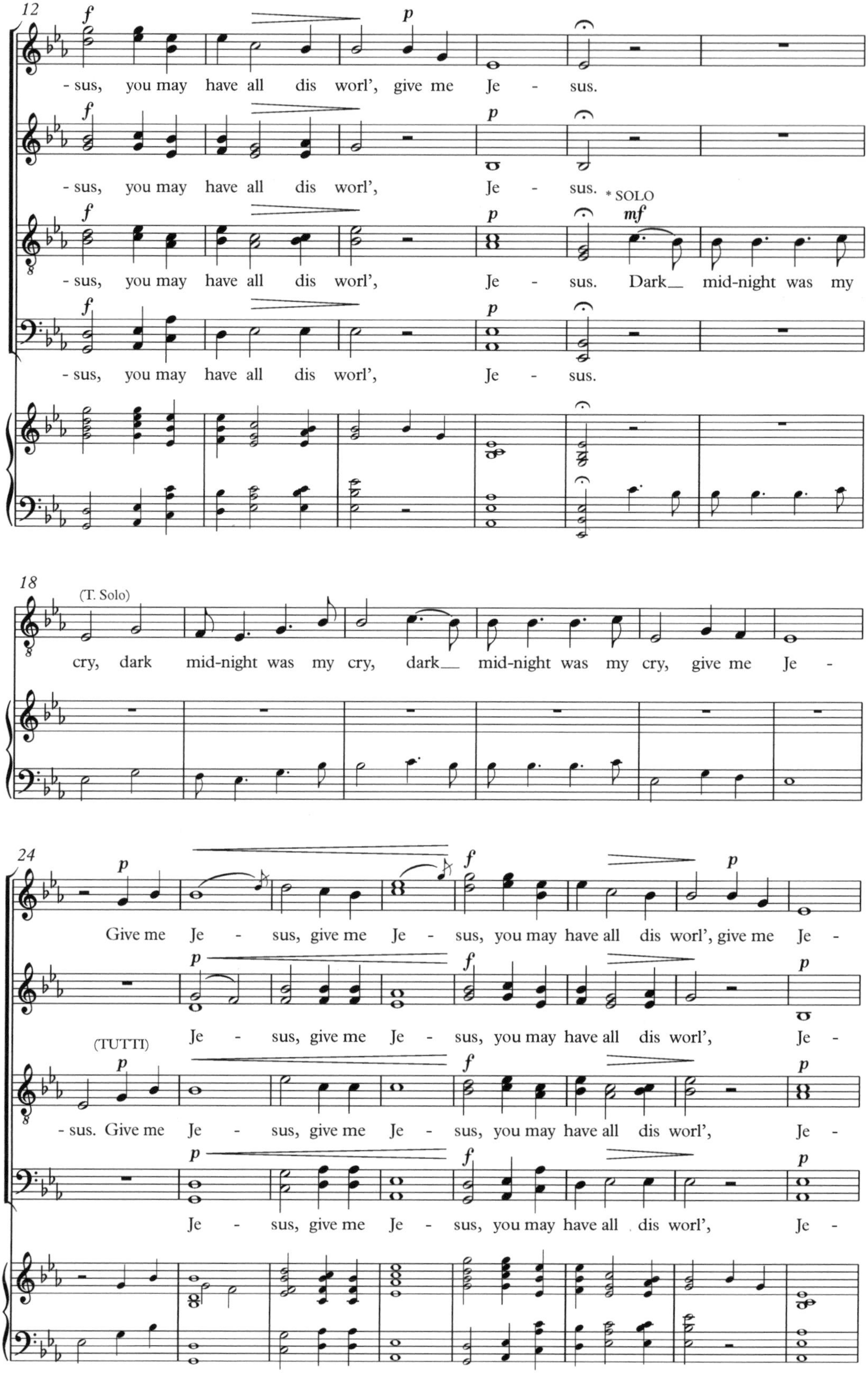

* Solos optional

NOVELLO REVISED STANDARD CHORAL EDITIONS

Fully revised and edited performing versions of many of the major works in the large-scale choral concert repertoire, replacing the standard Novello editions, often putting back the composers' intentions, restoring the original text, modernised accompaniments and providing new English translations. **Orchestral material, where necessary, is available on hire.**

J.S. BACH
(ed. Neil Jenkins)

Ascension Oratorio
NOV090860
German and English text

Christmas Oratorio
NOV072500
German and English text

Easter Oratorio
NOV090849
German and English text

Magnificat in D and E♭
NOV072529
German and English text in the
four Lauds in the E♭ version

Mass in B minor
NOV078430

St. John Passion
NOV072489
German and English text

St. Matthew Passion
NOV072478
German and English text

BEETHOVEN
(ed. Michael Pilkington)

**Choral Finale
to the Ninth Symphony**
NOV072490
German and English text

Mass in C NOV078560

Missa Solemnis (Mass in D)
NOV072497

BRAHMS
(ed. Pilkington)

A German Requiem
NOV072492
German and English text

DVOŘÁK
(Pilkington)

Mass in D NOV072491

Requiem NOV072516

Stabat Mater NOV072503

Te Deum NOV078573

ELGAR
(ed. Bruce Wood)

The Dream of Gerontius
NOV072530

Great is the Lord
NOV320067

Te Deum and Benedictus
NOV320078

GOUNOD
(Pilkington)

**Messe solennelle de
Sainte Cécile** NOV072495

HANDEL

Alexander's Feast
(ed. Donald Burrows)
NOV070446

Belshazzar
(Burrows) NOV070530

Dixit Dominus
(ed. Watkins Shaw)
NOV072323

Four Coronation Anthems
NOV072507
  The King Shall Rejoice
  (ed. Damian Cranmer)
  Let Thy Hand be Strengthened
  (Burrows)
  My Heart is Inditing
  (Burrows)
  Zadok the Priest
  (Burrows)

Judas Maccabaeus
(ed. Merlin Channon)
NOV072486

The King Shall Rejoice
(Cranmer) NOV072496

**Let Thy Hand be
Strengthened** *(Burrows)*
NOV072509

Messiah *(Shaw)* NOV070137
Study Score NOV090074

My Heart is Inditing
(Burrows)
NOV072508

**O Praise the Lord (from
Chandos Anthem No. 9)**
(ed. Graydon Beeks) NOV072511

Samson (complete) *(Burrows)*
NOV090926
Full score NOV078903

This is the Day *(Burrows)*
NOV072510

Zadok the Priest *(Burrows)*
NOV290704

HAYDN
(Pilkington)

The Creation NOV072485
German and English text

The Seasons NOV072493
German and English text

Te Deum Laudamus
NOV078463

"Maria Theresa" Mass
NOV078474

Mass "In Time of War"
NOV072514

"Nelson" Mass NOV072513

"Wind Band" Mass
(Harmoniemesse) NOV078507

MAUNDER

Olivet to Calvary
NOV072487

MENDELSSOHN
(Pilkington)

Elijah NOV070201
German and English text

Hymn of Praise
NOV072506

MOZART

Requiem
(ed. Duncan Druce) NOV070529

**Coronation Mass
(Mass in C K.317)**
(Pilkington) NOV072505

Mass in C minor
(reconstr. Philip Wilby)
NOV078452

ROSSINI

Petite messe solennelle
NOV072436

SCHUBERT

**Mass in G, D.167
(SSA version)**
NOV070258

SCHÜTZ
(Jenkins)

Christmas Story
NOV072525
German and English text

STAINER
(Pilkington)

The Crucifixion
NOV072488

VERDI
(Pilkington)

Requiem
NOV072403

VIVALDI
(ed. Jasmin Cameron)

Gloria
NOV078441